How R Arrived in England

Written and illustrated by
Ginge Brown

A **Moving On** Book

unsung heroes
Winners of The Queen's Golden Jubilee Award 2003

Editor
Liz Beer

Publisher Robert Dawson/Derbyshire Gypsy Liaison Group

989900633147

Publisher Robert Dawson
on behalf of Derbyshire Gypsy Liaison Group
188 Alfreton Road, Blackwell,
Alfreton, Derbys. DE55 5JH

ISBN 1-903418-33-X

CA: KS1 and 2
RA: 9y 9m (but artificially high)

The rights of Ginge Brown to be identified as the author and illustrator has been asserted in accordance with the Copyright Designs and Patents Act 1988. All rights reserved. Other than for normal review purposes, no part of this publication may be reproduced, transmitted or stored in a retrieval system, in any form by any means, without permission in writing through the Publisher.

Series Editor: Robert Dawson

Printed by 4 Sheets Design and Print Ltd.
197 Mansfield Road, Nottingham, NG1 3FS

Acknowledgement

Grateful thanks to Liz Beer for editing and to the various TESs who requested traditional stories.

Derbyshire Gypsy Liaison Group acknowledges with gratitude funding assistance given by the Esmee Fairbairn Foundation and by the Tudor Trust without whom these books would not have been possible.

How Rabbits Arrived in England... ...The Story

This is a story my Great Great Auntie told us. Us was me, my brothers and my sisters. It was the nineteen sixties. She was about eighty years old then.

A long time ago a tribe of Kalderash Romanes left a country called Austria. They travelled across Europe. Their leader was called Moses and he led his tribe to Holland.

There weren't many people in his tribe. There were two families with six adults and eleven children. When they got to Holland they sold their horses and their mules. They kept their tents.

They chartered a small boat to take them across the sea. The captain told them not to bring any animals with them. They sold their juckels (dogs) and all the other animals they had.

But Moses, the leader, took two young boys, named Ephraim and Jacob, aside. He told them to keep four young rabbits. They were to hide them very carefully. Moses said that nobody was to find them.

The tribe soon arrived in the North of England. No one found the rabbits.

The families settled down quickly. It wasn't long before they acquired more horses. They began travelling around the countryside.

The boys had looked after the rabbits well. Soon there were more and more rabbits. Jacob and Ephraim collected grass and other food as they travelled. The rabbits needed a lot to eat.

One day Jacob asked Moses why they had bothered to bring the rabbits with them. Moses told the boys that the rabbits were for food. They had brought them in case there were no rabbits in England.

Moses was right because there wasn't one rabbit in England. Jacob and Ephraim had brought the very first rabbits from across the sea.

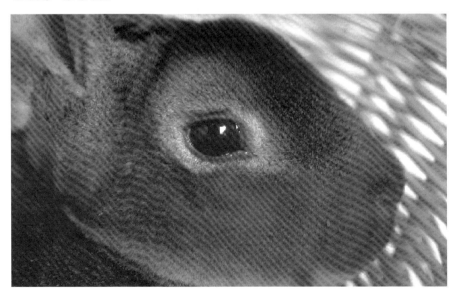

There were now over twenty rabbits. The two boys were struggling to find enough food for them to eat.

One day they were collecting food in a field of carrots. The farmer caught them. He asked them what they were doing. They told him they were collecting food for rabbits.

He thought they were lying. The farmer had never heard of an animal called a rabbit before.

He took them to the police station. The police hadn't heard of rabbits either. The two boys were taken back to their people. They were fined a penny for stealing carrots.

The tribe was forced to move on. They travelled a couple of miles. Then they set up their tents in a wood.

That evening Moses called the two boys over to him. They thought they would be beaten for getting caught. Instead old Moses said he had a plan to make the farmer sorry for not believing the boys.

He told the boys to get one male rabbit and four females and take them back to the carrot field.

And yes, you've guessed it. He told the boys to release them in the carrot field.

The farmer soon realised what rabbits were.

And that is the story of how rabbits came to England.

How Rabbits Arrived in England...
...The Play

Characters:
- Story teller
- Moses
- Captain
- Jacob
- Ephraim
- Farmer
- Police officer

Storyteller

Once upon a time some Kalderash Romanes left Austria. They travelled across Europe. Moses was their leader. He took them to Holland.

Moses

We are going to charter a boat and go to England. We will have to sell our wagons and horses. We will keep the tents and take them with us.

Storyteller

The tribe wasn't a big one. There were only two families — six grown ups and eleven children.

Moses
Captain, we would like to charter your boat to go to England.

Captain
Well you can but you cannot take any animals on board with you.

Moses

Thank you, Captain. We will go and sell the rest of our animals now.

Storyteller

So they got rid of all their juckels and other animals. But Moses took two young boys to one side and whispered to them.

Moses

Jacob, Ephraim, go and find four little rabbits. Hide them very carefully. Go on board the boat. Make sure no one finds them.

Storyteller

Jacob and Ephraim found four little rabbits and hid them. The boat took the tribe to the North of England. No one found the rabbits and the tribe landed safely. The families settled quickly. They bought more horses and travelled around the countryside.

Jacob

Come on Ephraim, we've got to get some more food for these rabbits. We've got twenty now.

Ephraim

They do eat a lot. They are getting bigger and bigger.

Jacob

I wonder why Moses wanted us to bring rabbits with us?

Ephraim

Let's ask Moses. He must have had a good reason.

Jacob

Moses, why did you want us to bring these rabbits to England?

Moses

Well I thought they would be good for food. And I wasn't sure there were any rabbits in England.

Jacob

We haven't seen any here at all. So maybe there weren't any before we came with ours.

Moses

I think these are the very first rabbits in England.

Ephraim

Come on, we've got to find more food. Look over there. It's a carrot field. I bet they'll eat carrots.

Jacob
We'll catch you up, Moses. We'll get a sackful and that will last us a few days.

Storyteller
The boys went into the field and started pulling up carrots and putting them in a sack.

Farmer
What are you boys doing?

Ephraim
Collecting carrots…

Jacob
To feed our rabbits…

Farmer

Rabbits — never heard of them before. I think you are fibbing to me. Come on, we are going to the police station. You can tell them your story.

Storyteller

The farmer took the boys to the police station. The police didn't believe them either.

Police officer

Rabbits — no such thing as rabbits. Let's find your family and see what they say.

Storyteller

The boys went with the policeman and found their families.

Police officer

Right now. It's a penny fine for these two boys stealing carrots and I want to see you gone by tonight. You can't stay here any longer.

Storyteller

The tribe moved on and set up camp in a wood two miles on. They set up their tents amon the trees.

Moses

Ephraim! Jacob! Come here, I want to talk to you.

Jacob

We didn't mean to get caught.

Ephraim

Are you very angry?

Moses

No, no I'm not cross. I've got a plan to make that farmer sorry for not believing you about rabbits. What I want you to do is this. Take one male and four female rabbits back to the carrot field. Let them go and then come back here. That farmer will be sorry he didn't believe you.

Storyteller
　The farmer soon realised what rabbits were and what they did. And that is the story of how rabbits came to England.

THE END